THE

GOLF

LOVER'S
COMPANION

THE GOLF LOVER'S COMPANION

Copyright © Summersdale Publishers Ltd, 2011

Illustrations by Ian Baker

Summersdale Publishers Ltd
46 West Street
Chichester
West Sussex
PO19 1RP
UK

www.summersdale.com

Printed and bound by CPI Group (UK) Ltd, Croydon, CR0 4YY

ISBN: 978-1-84953-176-4

Substantial discounts on bulk quantities of Summersdale books are available to corporations, professional associations and other organisations. For details contact Summersdale Publishers by telephone: +44 (0) 1243 771107, fax: +44 (0) 1243 786300 or email: nicky@summersdale.com.

THE

GOLF

LOVER'S
COMPANION

Ben Fraser

Illustrations by Ian Baker

summersdale

Contents

INTRODUCTION

It is almost impossible to remember
how tragic a place this world is
when one is playing golf.

Robert Lynd

Many people think golf is all about cringe-worthy jumpers, oddly patterned socks and flimsy excuses to get together for a drink at the 19th: a bad round (commiseration), a good round (celebration), an average round (a bit of both); this book is for all of those who know that all this true, but love the game anyway.

There is, of course, so much more to this grand and noble sporting tradition than meets the eye. St Andrews is arguably one of the most famous sporting venues of all time, preserving a history that stretches back several hundred years. Today, pro golfers are sports superstars – even a caddie has a chance of earning a fortune if they're carrying a bag for someone like Tiger. Whether it's the Masters or a Saturday round with friends, drama, intrigue and a burning desire to win are almost always on the cards.

Golf isn't just about technical skill or competitive achievements, either. As Grantland Rice once said, 'Eighteen holes of match or medal play will teach you more about your foe than will 18 years of dealing with him across a desk.' Playing (and even watching) golf gives an insight into a player's psyche as they struggle to overcome the mental battle that rages when faced with a long putt or awkward lie – even if this only translates verbally in short sharp bursts of four-letter words.

Whether you regard golf as an escape, a sophisticated sport to be treated with the utmost seriousness, something you play with wonky putters at your hotel in Spain or just an excuse for some fresh air and a stroll, interrupted bit of light activity and occasional concentration, this witty and humorous miscellany will have something to amuse you – or at least distract you when you've spent your day hacking about in the cabbage and dodging branches. So without further ado, let's tee off...

Golf, like the measles, should be
caught young, for, if postponed to
riper years, the results may
be serious.

P. G. Wodehouse

Backswing to the Future

Golf was never meant to be an exact science. Einstein was lousy at it.

Bob Toski

A SLICE OF HISTORY

The question of when and where golf was invented is a difficult one to answer. Who can be sure of the exact moment that someone first used a stick to hit a ball into a hole?

Some historians have suggested the Roman game *paganica*, in which participants used a bent stick to hit a stuffed leather ball further than a smaller, heavier ball, was the original precursor to the game. Other evidence suggests that the Chinese game *chuiwan* was one of the first examples of a game similar to golf: a painting from the fifteenth century, showing the Ming Emperor Xuande holding a club-like implement, on a square pitch with flags marking holes into which a ball was driven, can be seen at the Forbidden City Museum in Beijing. As with many great inventions, it seems that a number of people across the globe had similar dreams of inventing an outdoor game involving skill, patience, a ball, some holes and something to hit the ball with. What we are sure of, however, is that golf in its modern form evolved largely from the game played in Scotland. The first written record of golf here appears in 1457 when King James II banned the sport as it apparently distracted the military from practising archery. No doubt he'd be slightly miffed to learn that today the Old Course at St Andrews is known as the 'home of golf'!

It seems that errors abound in the early history of golf – as H. V. Morton in his book *In Search of Scotland* notes, the gold medal given by William IV in 1837, to be played for as an annual prize at the club, bore the word 'golph' rather than 'golf', which Morton puts down to 'some uncivilised London goldsmith!'.

ANYONE FOR GOWF?

The word golf derives from the Scottish word *gowf*
which probably come from the Dutch word *kolf*
meaning 'bat' or 'club'. The popular idea that the
word golf is an acronym for 'Gentlemen Only, Women
Forbidden' is a common myth, as acronyms being used
as words is a relatively modern phenomenon.

GOLF: THE EARLY YEARS

1552 – The first recorded reference to golf at St Andrews.

1659 – The first known reference to golf in America. It gets banned! Well, from the streets of Albany, N.Y. at any rate.

1744 – The earliest recorded set of rules is created by the Honourable Company of Edinburgh Golfers.

1811 – The first women's tournament is held in Musselburgh, Scotland. The prize for winning is a small fishing basket.

1873 – The Claret Jug is first awarded as the prize for winning The Open Championship (often referred to incorrectly as the British Open, especially on the other side of the Atlantic).

1916 – North Carolina opens the first standardised miniature golf course at Pinehurst – it was called Thistle Dhu (This'll Do) and was designed to satisfy the need for golf when time, space and money were in short supply.

Golf is a day spent in a round of
strenuous idleness.

William Wordsworth

The uglier a man's legs are, the
better he plays golf. It's almost
a law.

H. G. Wells

V IS FOR VARDON

During the pre-war years, Harry Vardon won The Open a record six times and was the most famous of a trio of golfers known as 'the great triumvirate' including J. H. Taylor and James Braid. Apart from his record number of wins, Vardon's biggest contribution to the game of golf is probably the 'Vardon grip', which most golfers use today. However, it is likely that Vardon did not actually invent this himself; at least one other player is thought to have used the grip long before. It was undoubtedly Vardon who popularised it, however, and made it a mainstay within the game.

THE FAIREST ON THE FAIRWAY

Lew Worsham stood over his golf ball on the 18th hole of the Jacksonville Open. If he could sink his ball in two shots then he had won the tournament and the $10,000 prize. He lined his putter up and set himself for his shot. Suddenly, he looked up, dropped his putter and walked over to the official.

'I touched the ball,' he admitted, 'call a penalty stroke.'

He then walked back and sunk his ball in the two shots that would previously have given him the win, but now left him tied for first place. He went on to lose the play-off but was hailed as a hero of sportsmanship and is more remembered for this loss than for his 1947 U.S. Open victory.

It's good sportsmanship not to pick
up lost balls while they are
still rolling.

Mark Twain

... golf may well be included
in that category of intolerable
provocations which may legally
excuse or mitigate behaviour not
otherwise excusable.

A.P. Herbert

FAMOUS GOLFER – 'YOUNG' TOM MORRIS
(1851–1875)

Born in St Andrews, 'Young' Tom Morris was perhaps the first star of professional golf. His father Old Tom Morris was greenkeeper and professional at St Andrews and then Prestwick, where young Tom attended the nearby Ayr Academy with the sons of noblemen and businessmen, but he was destined to be a golfer and would not waste time getting there. At thirteen, he beat his father, then The Open Champion, in a friendly game and a few years later he was gaining the attention of professional players for his natural talent, winning a play-off in a major tournament at Carnoustie at just sixteen years of age.

Tom was responsible more than any other player at the time for thrusting the sport into the public eye thanks to his vigour, charisma and the innovations he brought to the game. By 1868, at the age of seventeen, he won his first championship belt and kept hold of it for the next two years. In fact, the rule was that three consecutive wins meant you were given the red Moroccan leather belt permanently, so it was Tom's to keep. This left the organisers without a trophy, so the Claret Jug was created for the next tournament and is still in use today. His matches attracted thousands of spectators.

Unfortunately Tom's reign at the pinnacle of golf was short-lived, though not through the fault of a waning talent. It was whilst playing an exhibition match in 1875 that Tom was given word that his wife was at grave risk during childbirth. With two holes remaining, he finished and won the match, but when he returned home his wife and newborn child were dead. Three months later, on Christmas day, 'Young' Tom Morris died, aged only twenty-four. The reason for his death is said to have been heart failure, with speculation that it was brought on by a broken heart.

Bob Ferguson, a fellow golfer and friend, provided a comment that brilliantly illustrates Tom's character and talent.

'Time and time again,' he said, 'Tommy would make his putt and watch the ball progress towards the hole with the words to his caddie, "Pick it out the hole, laddie".'

A HOLE LOTTA LOVE

All golfers blame chance for
other accidents, but accept full
responsibility when they hit a
hole-in-one.

Alan Blackwell

LITTLE WHITE BALLS

Everyone knows what a modern-day golf ball looks like, but its current form was a long time coming. Wooden balls were the first to be used, in the seventeenth century, followed by stuffed leather balls known as 'featheries'. Chicken and goose feathers were boiled down so they could be stitched up into a ball using cowhide, and this became standard equipment for two centuries. It was not until the late 1800s that American Coburn Haskell came upon a new idea by chance, having wound a long piece of rubber thread into a ball while waiting for his golfing partner one day. After adding a cover and fine-tuning the length of the rubber twine used, Haskell had the first modern golf ball. With the development of durable synthetic materials like urethane, which allows balls to be built up in layers, the golf ball took its final flight into the item we know today. The window for someone to invent a rough-repelling, bunker-avoiding ball that ensures the perfect shot every time is, however, still open.

BIRDIE-SPOTTING

Golf has some inventive ways of describing a player's performance. Here's a list of some of the game's bird-inspired terminology:

BIRDIE – One under (Very good)

EAGLE – Two under (Excellent)

ALBATROSS (DOUBLE EAGLE) – Three under (Fantastic)

CONDOR – Four under (Unbelievably rare)

OSTRICH – Five under (Next to impossible, as it requires a par-6 hole, which is rare)

PHOENIX – Six under (Even more unlikely than an 'ostrich', because a par-7 hole is hardly ever seen and it would be even longer than a par-6 hole if it was)

LITTLE BLACK HOLES

Like many standards in golf, the rule about the size of the holes on a course came from the founding fathers at the Royal and Ancient Golf Club of St Andrews. It was agreed that a consistent size from course to course was necessary, along with other rules for the sake of competition, as the game increased in popularity. It may be that the 4.25 in. standard was decided as a result of the only existing hole-cutter being made to that size; some say the original hole-cutter was simply a length of drainage pipe, hence the predetermined diameter. Whichever the case, a depth of at least 4 inches was also agreed and the specification was introduced into the rules in 1891. The first purpose-built hole-cutter can be viewed today at the Royal Musselburgh course in Prestonpans, Scotland.

CATCHING A BOGEY

Although used regularly in today's game to denote 'one over par', the term 'bogey' has a curious and unlikely origin. According to the United States Golf Association (USGA), the use of the word 'bogey' in golf can be traced back to a song called 'The Bogey Man', popular in the British Isles in the 1890s. The song contains the line, 'I'm the Bogey Man, catch me if you can'– bogeyman having been used for centuries to mean a mysterious and imaginary monster – thus, when golfers sought that elusive perfect score, they would often refer to it as chasing a 'bogey'.

GREAT GOLF FACTS

Sixty-seven million to one are the reputed odds of getting two holes-in-one in a round of golf. Let's just say it's a long shot.

- A standard golf ball has 336 dimples but they can have anywhere from 300 to 500 and the record holder has an amazing 1,070 little dimples.

- The water at the 17th hole on the Stadium Course at Sawgrass, Florida swallows 125,000 golf balls a year. That's a hungry lake.

- In 2010 Japanese company TourStage produced a range of coloured golf balls – V10 – including 'Super Yellow' ones which are said to have a calming influence, as well as being easy to spot. Not an original idea by any means, but they may be one of the first to introduce the grass-coloured golf ball. Why anyone would want a ball that is harder to see while playing is anybody's guess.

It would have been a birdie if
the ball hadn't stopped before it
reached the hole.

David Coleman

I played so good today it was like
the hole kept getting in the way of
my ball.

Calvin Peete after winning the
Greater Milwaukee Open

GOLF AROUND THE WORLD

Golf is the easiest game in the
world to play. You just hit the ball
and then swear.

Sid Caesar

There are reputed to be 60–100 million regular golfers in the world. The exact number is hard to determine but there are certainly a lot of people playing a lot of golf. But what constitutes a regular golfer: a round per week, a few hits on the driving range, a bit of putting practice, or every day spent sinking eighteen on the greens?

Certainly in some countries it is difficult for golf lovers to play as much as they would like. Aside from having access to the equipment, one also needs access to a course. There are around 32,000 golf courses worldwide, but is that enough to cater for the demand? In Japan, for instance, it is difficult to find the space to open new courses, especially in densely built-up areas. This results in some big waiting lists and some very expensive rounds of golf.

MOST GOLF COURSES PER CAPITA: excluding countries with less than 500,000 people:

1. Scotland
2. New Zealand
3. Australia
4. Republic of Ireland
5. Northern Ireland
6. Canada
7. Wales
8. United States
9. Sweden
10. England

KOREAN MASTERS

While the European Tour has been held in China, India, Malaysia, Indonesia, Singapore, Thailand and Hong Kong, golf is still a rare sport across much of Asia. In South Korea, however, golf is already something akin to a religion. The playing population is estimated at around four million, or one in twelve. The semi-tropical island of Jeju to the south, well known as a honeymoon destination and for its natural beauty, also has no fewer than twenty-three golf courses. South Korea's K. J. Choi is Asia's most successful player, while South Koreans are a strong presence in the top ranks of the women's game. Golf took off in South Korea in the late 1990s after the country's economic boom, when Se Ri Pak won two majors in her debut US LPGA season. The KPGA has more than 800 full-time professionals and 500 teaching professionals.

OUT OF AFRICA

Golf may not be the first thing that comes to mind when thinking of Africa, but the sport does in fact have a strong following there; what's more, it has been combined with the more classic recreation of safari – meaning that golfers can hunt for glimpses of Africa's native wildlife when they've had enough of hunting for their balls. Most 'golf safaris' simply combine a standard grass course with a habitat suitable for giraffes, hippos and crocodiles, often combined further with savannah views and glowing skies. The Jinja golf course in Uganda is famous for having a rule that allows a player a free drop if the ball lands in a hippo's footprint. Play is also stopped if any elephants wander onto the course. Fly over to the Fajara Club in The Gambia for an altogether more wild experience – fairways resemble dried riverbeds that wind through dense bushland, temperatures can verge on the unbearable and their 'greens' are actually 'browns', consisting of oil sand and for which a 'brown-sweeper' will come in handy.

A TASTE OF ANCIENT MOROCCO

If you fancy a golf experience with a little ancient-world flavour, why not try the Amelkis Golf Club in Marrakech. It features a Kasbah-like clubhouse and an eleventh-century irrigation system and many of its holes are lined with age-old palms and giant papyrus reeds. Fez optional.

CHINESE DEMOCRACY

At the time of writing the largest golfing facility in the world, The Mission Hills Golf Club in Shenzhen, China, has an amazing twelve courses, each designed by a prominent person in the golfing world.

1. World Cup Course: Jack Nicklaus, United States
2. Norman Course: Greg Norman, Australia
3. Annika Course: Annika Sörenstam, Sweden
4. Els Course: Ernie Els, South Africa
5. Vijay Course: Vijay Singh, Fiji
6. Faldo Course: Nick Faldo, England
7. Olazábal Course: José María Olazábal, Spain
8. Duval Course: David Duval, United States
9. Ozaki Course: Jumbo Ozaki, Japan
10. Leadbetter Course: David Leadbetter, England
11. Pete Dye Course: Pete Dye, United States
12. Zhang Lianwei Course: Zhang Lianwei, China

WAY OUT BACK

There are some expansive golf courses out there; some can take all day and maybe more to meander around. There is one golf course, however, that stands out amongst the rest. The Nullarbor Links course in Australia is a staggering 848 miles long. It is an 18-hole par-72 golf course with an average of 50 miles between each hole. Situated along the desolate Eyre Highway across Western and South Australia, it spans two time zones. The time it takes to complete will depend on your driving (on the course and on the road) but four days is the recommended duration. There are cafés and hotels along the way to break up the trip and each person who finishes the course receives a certificate confirming they have completed the longest golf course in the world. I don't think anyone would begrudge you a stop at the nineteenth after that!

MONKEY BUSINESS

The island of Tonga only has one golf course but if you happen to play there and a monkey steals your ball, don't panic, because the rules state you won't receive a penalty.

GOLFING LUNAR-CY

The first and only man to have played golf on the moon is Alan Shepard. It was on 6 February 1971 when the NASA astronaut decided to take extreme golfing to a new level. He apparently smuggled the head of a 6 iron and a couple of golf balls on board the mission inside his spacesuit. (Why not!) Then after landing he attached the Wilson head to a lunar sample scoop handle, thereby constructing his very own club. Due to the restrictiveness of his gloves and spacesuit, he could only use one hand to swing the club. After a couple of scrappy shots he got a good hit and sent the ball, as he put it, 'miles and miles and miles'. The ball is still out there somewhere.

The world's number one tennis player spends ninety per cent of his time winning, while the world's number one golfer spends ninety per cent of his time losing.

David Feherty

In Ireland the nineteenth hole is mandatory, as are twenty and twenty-one.

Bill Murray

PIONEERS AND PETTICOATS

Golf is a game of coordination, rhythm and grace; women have these to a high degree.

Babe Zaharias

QUEEN OF SCOTS

Mary, Queen of Scots was apparently the first woman to play golf in Scotland. Famous paintings of the time show her strolling across the green with her then-husband Lord Darnley, followed by dozens of courtiers. So passionate was she about the game that she earned a rebuke from the church for enjoying a round of golf only months after Lord Darnley's death, with his supposed murderer, the Earl of Bothwell. It seems that the good Queen wasn't above a bet or two on the green, as one story of the time has her losing a lavishly jewelled necklace to her lady-in-waiting Mary Seton.

WORDS FROM SOME FEMALE
HALL-OF-FAMERS

Judy Bell (Lifetime Achievement) – 'Golf is for everyone regardless of race, colour or physical handicaps.'

Donna Caponi (Veteran Category) – 'I owe everything to my dad, who spent hours and hours and hours teaching me.'

Dorothy Campbell Hurd Howe (Original Pinehurst member) – '[The short game] is almost second nature to me.'

Betsy King – 'Forget what is behind and press toward what is ahead, toward the goal to win the prize.'

Dinah Shore (from Pinehurst) – 'Ability is the only thing that matters.'

SOMETHING FISHY

One of the original women's golf competitions was
between the Musselburgh 'Fish Ladies' in 1810. They
used to stage competitions on Shrove Tuesday between
the 'marrieds' and the 'unmarrieds', and by all
accounts it was the 'marrieds' that used to
take the day.

If a woman can walk, she can play golf.

Louise Suggs

I'll take a two-shot penalty but I'll be damned if I'm going to play the ball where it lies.

Elaine Johnson in 1982 after her tee shot rebounded
off a tree and ended up in her bra

GONE FISHIN'

Although some people might, upon shooting the ball into a river, accept a penalty shot and play three from the tee, Mrs Meehan was not of their number. In 1913 the good lady hit an unfortunate shot from the tee of the short sixteenth, landing smack in the middle of the Binniekill River. Not one to be daunted, or take the logical solution, Mrs Meehan grabbed a nearby boat and rowed furiously after her ball. We can only assume that boats were often left lying around the golf courses in Shawnee, Pennsylvania. After a mile she caught up with the ball and started to attempt to chip it back onto dry land by hanging over the side. She succeeded after a mere thirty-nine shots, chipping it onto the bank, a mile and a half from the green, and chose to golf her way back to the hole, where, 119 shots later, she sank her putt.

FAMOUS GOLFER: BABE ZAHARIAS (1911–1956)

Except perhaps for Arnold Palmer, no golfer has ever been more
beloved by the gallery.

Charles McGrath, *The New York Times* journalist,
on Babe Zaharias

Mildred Ella Didrikson Zaharias, better known as 'Babe Zaharias',
was an American athlete par excellence who, in her varied sporting
career, won Olympic medals for track and field, led an Amateur
Athletics Union basketball team and competed in some of golf's
biggest tournaments, breaking records and breaking boundaries
for women athletes everywhere in the process.

Born in Port Arthur, Texas, to immigrants from Norway,
Mildred Didrikson was a keen sportswoman at school, excelling
in sports that were then considered by most to be 'for the boys'.
In one game of baseball Mildred hit five home runs – this, she
attested, was how she came to be known as 'Babe', after the
legendary slugger Babe Ruth. Already a budding renaissance

woman in her twenties, Babe could sing and play harmonica to a level that saw her record a number of songs with Mercury Records, including 'I Felt a Little Teardrop'. She also played competitive pool. After meeting the Greek-American wrestler George Zaharias in 1938, when – in another typically audacious move – she entered as the only woman in the men's Los Angeles Open, Babe fell in love and got married.

In a remarkable golfing career, to which she came late, she took forty-one Ladies Professional Golf Association (LPGA) wins, including four Western Opens and three U.S. Women's Opens. In 1950, she got a grand slam of three women's majors – the Western Open, the Titleholders Championship and the U.S. Open, a year in which she also became the fastest LPGA golfer to reach ten wins.

In 1951 Babe was inducted into the World Golf Hall of Fame, having established herself as a truly great golfer and perhaps the single-most outstanding female athlete the world had yet seen. At the age of forty-five, tragically, she lost her battle with cancer and left a golfing legacy that still shines today – she is remembered with her own park and museum, located in Beaumont, Texas.

RECORD BREAKERS

- The youngest female golfer to score a hole-in-one is Soona Lee-Tolley (USA), aged 5 years 103 days, at the par-3 7th at Manhattan Woods Golf Club, West Nyack, New York, USA, on 1 July 2007.

- The oldest female player to score her age is Kayoko Fukui (Japan, b. 5 October 1936), who scored 70 at Taiheiyo Golf Club, Karuizawa, Japan, on 16 August 2007.

- Female athletes competed in the Olympics for the first time at the 1900 Games held in Paris, France. Alongside the 975 male athletes, a total of twenty-two women competed for glory in sports such as tennis and golf.

THE 19TH HOLE

My favourite hole was always the
watering hole.

Ronan Rafferty

Whether your days are filled with birdies or bogeys, the clubhouse bar is the last port of call and the ideal repose after the day's events. The balls may not have been sinking well but to sink a drink takes no effort at all. The lounge will often hold a splendid view over the course, a perfect place to enjoy a tipple or two. Most will serve food but some of the smaller clubs may need prior notice to prepare a lunch or evening meal.

The clubhouse is the focal point of any golf club and may be steeped in tradition. It could be a good idea to research the protocol for dress beforehand; they are generally relaxed and friendly places but you wouldn't want to inadvertently offend anyone. One hard and fast rule is to change out of your golf shoes before entering. Metal or even soft spikes can damage the floor. There is usually a changing room where your golfing attire can be replaced by your social dress and where there are showers to freshen up. A number of clubhouses require you to wear a jacket and most of them would require you to remove your hat.

A feature of most clubhouses will be an honours board on the wall. This will display names of the past winners of various competitions, Club Champions and Captains. You may feel a nostalgic sense of history when perusing these wooden remnants of times past; indeed, some of them stretch back to the nineteenth century.

A man comes into the clubhouse and asks if anyone wants to hear a joke about golf pros. The barman says, 'Just so you know, the guy on your left is a former wrestler turned golf pro, the guy on your right is a boxer turned golf pro and I'm a hit man turned golf pro. Still want to tell the joke?' The man looks at them all and replies, 'Not if I'm going to have to explain it three times.'

GOLF-THEMED DRINK

Crooked Golf Cart

- 5 parts Cranberry Juice
- 1 part Amaretto
- 1 splash White Rum
- 2 slices Lime

Serve in a highball glass. Half fill the glass with crushed ice. Pour in cranberry juice and add the amaretto. Continue with the cranberry juice and throw a splash of white rum over the top. Then drink over two slices of fresh lime.

JIM THE LAD

Jimmy Demaret is considered by many to be golf's first showbiz celebrity. Renowned for his singing, joke telling, drinking and outlandish dress, he also carved out a reputation for his golfing ability and in his day was the star of the show. Between 1935 and 1957 he won thirty-one PGA Tour events, including the Masters three times, and he had a superb record in the Ryder Cup of 5–0. But he never lifted the U.S. Open. Aside from his flamboyant lifestyle he was especially known for his brilliant play in windy conditions. He died of a heart attack while preparing for a round of golf.

The nineteenth hole is the only one where players can have as many shots as they like.

Louis Safian

A young woman was on the green playing her first full round of golf after receiving lessons from a golf pro. It was a hot day and she was wearing shorts. She had only just begun when she was stung by a wasp. She was determined to carry on but the pain was quite severe, so she decided in the end to turn back. On entering the clubhouse she was approached by her golf pro who wanted to know why she was back so early.

'I was stung by a wasp and it hurt so much I had to finish my game,' she replied.

'Where?' He enquired.

'Between the first and second hole.'

He looked her up and down and nodded.

'I believe your stance may be too wide.'

You know you're a golfing fanatic when you prefer to play golf traditionally and have a shot of Scotch at each hole – your game doesn't improve, but strangely you don't seem to care.

GOLF-THEMED DRINK

Hole-in-One

- 1 oz Scotch
- 3/4 oz Vermouth
- 1/4 tsp Lemon Juice
- 1 dash Orange Bitters

Shake all the ingredients together and pour into a cocktail glass on ice. Why not drink it in the manner the name suggests?

Jeremy and Charles are having a pint in the clubhouse. Jeremy says, 'My wife is threatening to leave me if I don't give up golf.'

'But that's awful!' replies Charles. 'What are you going to do?'

Jeremy takes a large swig of beer, thoughtfully wipes the froth from his top lip, sighs, and replies, 'I'm going to miss her.'

DRINKING AND DRIVING

Golf has always had its star players, but for a long time it has also had players who are stars – a whole host of celebrities from the world of film and music have been and continue to be drawn to the game, and there are those odd few who loved to sink a few gins as much as they liked to sink a few putts. Who could forget old Dino, Dean Martin, who, when not indulging in one of his most favourite pastimes – wetting his whistle with a little something from the bar – liked nothing more than to play a round with his pal Frank? One man who could no doubt have given Martin a run for his money at the bar and on the green was hellraiser Ollie Reed, who was also known to be a great fan of the game. The Battle Golf Club, East Sussex, has one of its lounge bars named after the great man himself.

If you drink, don't drive. Don't even putt.

Dean Martin

What scoundrel took the cork out of my lunch?

W. C. Fields during a 'snack' break at the Lakeside
Club in LA

Arsenic.

Ben Crenshaw to a bartender who asked him what
he wanted to drink after he failed to qualify for The
Open Championship in 1992

Scotland is the birthplace of golf and salmon fishing. Which may explain why it is also the birthplace of whisky.

Henry Beard

BOTTLING IT

During the 1949 Open Championship Harry Bradshaw accidentally drove his ball into a beer bottle. The neck and shoulder broke but the ball still remained lodged within the bottle. Instead of taking a penalty he played the ball where it lay and smashed the bottle with his club. The ball travelled about 30 ft, and the bottle was no more.

What happened to the golfer whose tee shot went through the clubhouse window?

He was arrested for dangerous driving.

GOLF-THEMED DRINK

Sand Trap

- 0.5 oz. Lemon Juice

- 0.5 oz. Sweet Vermouth

- 1 oz. Cherry Brandy

- 1.5 oz. Scotch

Fill a shaker half full of ice then add the above ingredients and shake well. Put more ice into a highball glass then strain the previous mixture over the top and serve with a slice of lemon.

But if she forgave neither of them,
they would probably go on boozing
and golfing together, and saying
quite dreadful things about her,
and not care very much whether
she forgave them or not.

E. F. Benson

WHO'S YOUR CADDY?

The first thing to understand about caddying is that it's not brain surgery. It's much more complicated than that.

Lawrence Donegan

ORIGIN OF THE WORD 'CADDY'

If you're a fan of loose tea then you might associate this word with the little tin that sits up in the cupboard – derived from the eighteenth-century 'catty', in this context the word denoted a unit of weight. However, the use of term 'caddy' in golf has a more extensive history. Its origins lie in the French *cadet,* meaning 'youngest in the family'. It has been suggested by some that the word came to the bonnie land of Scots when, after having her clubs carried by military *cadets* in France, Queen Mary Stuart returned to Scotland in 1561.

According to records, the term first cemented its golf-specific meaning in 1857; paintings from this era also show caddies at work carrying bundles of clubs; no ergonomically designed wheelie bags in those days!

MORE THAN JUST A GOOD PAIR OF LEGS

In the modern game, the image of a caddy as a load-bearing lackey is completely out of date. The caddy today must perform according to a strict etiquette and can expect to be called upon to exercise expert knowledge on everything from reading greens to estimating weather variables. Modern caddies are also equipped with an array of equipment to assist their judgements, including yardage lasers to determine shot distances. The rules on the use of electronic aids in professional golf can vary – the USGA rules state that:

'Except as provided in the Rules, during a stipulated round the player must not use any artificial device or unusual equipment, or use any equipment in an unusual manner:

a. That might assist him in making a stroke or in his play; or

b. For the purpose of gauging or measuring distance or conditions that might affect his play.'

This would, one expects, include the use of yardage lasers, though a caddy could quite easily mark up distances in a notebook (which is generally permitted) before play begins. No doubt such gadgets can give some players a slight edge, though if a player is having a bad day, the only thing a yardage laser would be good for is calculating the distance to the bar at the clubhouse.

Our relationship lasted longer than either of his two marriages.

Nick Faldo's coach David Leadbetter, who was sacked by Faldo after thirteen years

I always know where a putt will break. It slopes towards the side of the green where Herman is standing.

Lee Trevino on his overweight caddy Herman Mitchell

CADDY OF A LIFETIME

Few caddies can claim to have earned a profile that could rival those of the players they assist, though long-serving Augusta caddy Carl Jackson has done just that. At the seventy-fifth Masters tournament in April 2011 Jackson made his fiftieth appearance caddying in the tournament, a career that began with him carrying his first bag at the same event in 1961, at the tender age of fourteen. At this time, when segregation still overshadowed the game, it was common for hopeful black men to take such a subservient role. However, through the years Jackson has acquired all but legendary status in the eyes of fans and golfers alike and is rightly hailed as 'as much a part of this place [Augusta] as the green jacket or Magnolia Lane'. Jackson's motto: the first rule of being a good caddy is being a good golfer.

BITS AND PIECES

- The course at Goodwood in West Sussex has motorised golf carts known as 'woodies', modelled on Lord Freddie March's 1934 Brakenvan, which, as many cars of the era did, featured wooden body panels.

- Actor Michael O'Keefe, who played the distracted adolescent caddy Danny Noonan in *Caddyshack* (1980), has since gone on to feature in no less than thirty film roles. He is also part of a group called The Peacemakers' Circle Foundation, which promotes 'socially engaged Buddhism'.

- Myles Byrne, sometime caddy to Ian Woosnam, dropped an almighty clanger when he cost his man a share of the lead in the final round of the 2001 Open Championship by loading his bag with fifteen clubs instead of the regulation fourteen. As such, Woosnam took a two-stroke penalty and ended up tied for third place. Byrne was duly dropped a couple of weeks later after he turned up late for the final round of the Scandinavian Masters.

- The one and only Che Guevara is known to have worked as a caddy in his homeland Argentina – he also played golf as a student.

LED BY LEADBETTER

He may be well known in the public eye as being the
long-time coach for Nick Faldo, but David Leadbetter,
originally from Worthing, West Sussex, has since
established himself as one of the world's leading
golf coaches. After having little luck as a player,
Leadbetter turned to instruction, building Faldo's
swing up to its championship-winning best. Although
not strictly a caddy, Leadbetter gave sterling advice
and was as close as could be to Faldo's game.

'Will you stop checking your watch every
five seconds, it's putting me off!' a golfer says
to his caddy.

'This isn't a watch, sir,' the caddy replies,
'it's a compass.'

After bumping four balls into the rough on the spin, I asked my caddy what I should take for my next shot. 'Either a cyanide capsule,' he replied, 'or the next plane home.'

Jack Lemmon

Taking the Rough with the Smooth

Everyone gets wounded in a game
of golf. The trick is not to bleed.

Peter Dobereiner

A couple of women were out golfing when one of them hit a wild shot into a group of men playing on another hole nearby. The woman who'd hit the wayward shot saw one of the men crumple into a heap with his hands between his legs, screaming in pain. She quickly ran over to apologise – 'Let me help you,' she said, 'I'm a physical therapist.'

'Yowch – I'll be alright in a minute,' the injured man said.

'Here,' the woman insisted, 'Let me help you,' and she promptly undid his flies and placed her hands inside his trousers. 'How does that feel?' she asked. 'Fantastic,' the man replied, 'but my thumb is still killing me!'

The provision of wild animals to enliven the game, to encourage agility in the players and relieve them of the charge of self-protectiveness, is a method which is at once more feasible and appeals to the sporting instincts of every true Briton.

The disappearance from our shores of bears, boars and wolves has confined animal risks on golf links. The time has come for an organised effort to provide them as regular features to the game.

C. L. Graves 1925

COURSE CALAMITIES

- Aussie golfer Scott Strange once fell foul to a killer grip – not his own, but that of a friend who greeted him with such a vigorous handshake that his tendons were left crushed.

- Whilst playing at Lundin Links in Scotland, Harold Wallace got hit by a train when crossing the track behind the 5th green.

- In the 1982 Singapore Open, Jim Stewart fell over a ten-foot cobra on the course. He managed to kill it but then stood back in shock as another snake slithered out of its mouth!

STRUCK DOWN IN THE PRIME OF YOUR SWING

Most golfers have heard the saying that you're more likely to be struck by lightning when playing golf than during any other activity, but is there any truth to this?

Well, if you play golf in the U.S. it may be far more likely than is desirable. The NLSI (National Lightning Safety Institute) published a report, based on thirty-five years of U.S. lightning statistics, documenting fatalities, injuries and damage. They found that twenty-seven per cent of instances occurred in open fields or recreational areas, whilst only five per cent occurred on golf courses. This may appear to let golf off the hook but when you think about how many people use open fields or recreational areas compared to golf courses then the outlook isn't so rosy. In fact, it leaves the golf course as by far the most likely place to be struck by lightning.

So next time there is a storm try not to be out in the open, standing on damp grass and holding a metal pole skywards – but be even more careful if you're playing golf!

I heard some good news today. Ten golfers a year are hit by lightning.

George Carlin

Any time you feel the urge to golf, instead take eighteen minutes and beat your head against a good solid wall. This is guaranteed to duplicate to a tee the physical and emotional beating you would have suffered playing a round.

Mark Oman

DEATH BY GOLF BALL

With all the shanks, flubs, rope hooks, muffs and yanks occurring on golf courses worldwide, it seems incredible that obituaries aren't continually filled with the phrase, 'death by golf ball'. Fortunately, there seem to be few recorded fatalities by a mishit golf ball, but it is not unheard of. In 2009 a grandmother was killed on a Scottish course when her son-in-law mishit his tee shot.

Always remember to stand behind and to the side of a player when they are teeing off and to shout 'fore' on those very rare occasions that you mishit a shot!

SET A COURSE FOR... THE COURSE

It's worth keeping half an eye looking skyward whilst playing golf, not only to spot any wayward golf balls but also any wayward aeroplanes!

On a course in Dundee, golfers were startled when a light aircraft crash-landed into a tree on the 15th hole. The pilot had started having difficulty whilst flying over the course so, taking inspiration from a Biggles story he had read as a child, he decided to execute a 'pancake' landing and drop flat into the top of a tree.

FORE... BY FOUR

Golf courses often create a variety of obstacles for golfers to navigate but it is easy to imagine the shock felt by course workers when they discovered a heavy-duty four-by-four vehicle in one of the bunkers. They were even more surprised when they looked inside and saw a couple of pirates in the back.

The police and paramedics were immediately called and soon determined what had happened. The pirates had been returning from a rather drunken party the previous evening when they decided to take an impromptu short cut across the golf course. Fortunately no one was hurt; it seems that after being shipwrecked the unfortunate pirates had simply fallen asleep.

BEING COURSE CONSCIOUS

Players are generally expected to take action to help preserve the playable condition of the course; hence one is expected to cap any divots created by carefully replacing the turf, and to rake over sand traps if you've been unfortunate enough to find yourself 'at the beach'.

A ROUGH RIDE

Golf carts have become hugely popular over the years for getting around film studios, airports and even schools. Unfortunately this leads to injuries – up to 30 per cent of them among children under sixteen.

On islands in the southern states of America, Belize and Hong Kong, where motor vehicles are restricted, residents have taken to using golf carts instead. In one retirement community in Florida, it's the most popular form of transport.

The problem is that they were never designed for safety and this has led to a huge number of accidents. Their small wheels and light framework make them very unstable and susceptible to tipping over. This doesn't stop thrill-seekers from using them as an alternative to the All-Terrain Vehicles they can't have in the first place.

Isn't a round of golf thrilling enough?

A man stumbles into the clubhouse with a broken nose, multiple bruises and a 9 iron embedded in his head. His friend looks across at him in amazement and asks what happened.

'Well,' says the man, 'I was playing a round of golf with my wife and on the seventh hole she hit a horrendous slice, sending her ball flying into a nearby field of cows. I gallantly climbed into the field with her and after searching the field for a few minutes spotted something white on the rear end of one of the cows. I went over to investigate and, sure enough, there was my wife's golf ball, stuck right in the middle of the cow's rear end. That's when I made my big mistake.'

'Why, what happened?' replied his friend.

'I lifted the cow's tail and shouted to my wife, "hey, this looks like yours!"'

I'd like to see the fairways more narrow. Then everyone would have to play from the rough, not just me.

Seve Ballesteros

No problem, Greg. You don't need to talk. Just listen.

Lee Trevino to an exasperated Greg Norman, who had said to him, 'Do you mind if we don't talk during the game today?'

FAMOUS GOLFER: JACK NICKLAUS (1940–)

God never gives it all to one person –
except maybe Jack Nicklaus.
Lee Trevino

Nicknamed 'The Golden Bear', owing to his then golden-blonde hair and stocky frame, Jack Nicklaus is one of pro golf's most revered legends.

Born in Ohio, he shot 51 in his first 9-hole round of golf at the age of ten. During his heyday in the sixties and seventies, he won at least one PGA Tour event in seventeen consecutive years.

In 1962 Nicklaus had his first major win, the U.S. Open, beating Arnold Palmer and sparking what was to become a long-running rivalry, although he has said: 'I never went into a tournament or round of golf thinking I had to beat a certain player. I had to beat the golf course.' After this the career milestones kept on coming: he was the first player to win the Masters twice in a row (1965 and 1966), he smashed Bobby Jones' record of thirteen major victories by racking up a total of seventeen himself by 1980, and then added one more when he became the Masters' oldest winner at the age of forty-six, just one and a half months younger than Old Tom Morris had been when he won The Open Championship 119 years earlier. Jones credits Nicklaus' 1965 Masters win as 'the greatest performance in all of golfing history'. Nicklaus has also finished first on the Senior PGA/Champions Tour ten times.

Jack was renowned for his straight and solid drives – he held the official PGA longest-drive title for over twenty years after reaching 312 metres in 1963. He is also a heavy hitter off the course, having regularly topped *Golf Inc.* magazine's 'Most Powerful people in Golf' list thanks to his business brand of equipment and instructional videos (the latest offering being an app with rangefinders, scorecards, statistical tracking and swing tutorials) and his involvement in developing and designing courses throughout the world. Nicklaus truly is golf's golden boy and has been woven into the very fabric of the game – and understandably so. He played 154 consecutive majors between 1957 and 1998, his last being The Open Championship at St Andrews in 2005.

JUGS, JACKETS AND JARGON

There's too much fussiness in golf clubs. I was asked to leave my last one because my socks weren't colour coordinated with my umbrella.

Mildred Sassoon

THE ART OF TRADITION

To many, golf might seem unnecessarily caught up in traditions, especially when it comes to some of the less fashionable articles of dress (who, other than the beaming Masters champion, could pull off a green jacket?). However, honouring old-fashioned ways of doing things is an important part of the game and helps to keep the sport unique. Here's a list of golfing traditions minor and major:

THE RULES – the birthplace of the modern game – the Royal and Ancient Golf Club of St Andrews (the R&A) – is still responsible for regulating the rules of the game everywhere, except in America where the United States Golf Association (USGA) performs the role.

LOVELY JUG-LY – the winner of The Open Championship is awarded a silver Claret Jug, carrying on a tradition first started in 1873. The original was first presented to Tom Kidd, as it wasn't ready in time to be presented to Young Tom Morris the year before, although his name was the first to be engraved on it; it is on display at the R&A. The current Claret Jug was first awarded in 1928.

MASTER OF THE MENU – all previous winners are invited to a champions' dinner each year at the Masters, the menu for which is decided upon by the reigning champion. This was begun by Ben Hogan in 1952, and in 1998 a twenty-two-year-old Tiger Woods served up a menu of cheeseburgers and milkshakes. By 2006, his tastes had turned to Mexican food: quesadillas with salsa, steak fajitas, refried beans – and the somewhat less Mexican apple pie and ice cream.

DONALD, WHERE'S YOUR TROOSERS?

The full-length tartan trousers worn today are based on traditional Scots trews, but cut fuller for more freedom of movement and warmer climates. The tartan plus fours, like long knickerbockers, which predated them were often worn with argyle knee socks.

AMEN CORNER

The part of the course where players encounter the water hazards on the second half of the 11th and 12th and first half of the 13th holes at Augusta has, since the phrase was coined by sports writer Herbert Warren Wind in 1958, become known as 'Amen Corner'. Wind puts the reference down to a song title – 'Shouting in that Amen Corner' by Milton Mezzrow – that occurred to him when he was thinking of a way to describe the miraculous efforts of Arnold Palmer, which proved decisive in the player's victory that year. It was later revealed that jazz historian Richard Moore had researched the reference and found that, in fact, the record didn't exist, suggesting Wind had actually meant the record of the same name, featuring Mildred Bailey. Despite Wind's minor inaccuracy, however, this part of the course is still referred to in this way, and is recognised as being somewhere players will either be thanking God for his blessings or praying for divine intervention.

Any golfer whose ball hits a seagull shall be said to have scored a birdie.

Frank Muir

Why is it called a three wood when it's made out of metal?

Ernie Witham

WORD GAMES

Golf has a reputation for being a gentlemanly sport – and rightly so as it's steeped in proud tradition. However, this has sometimes meant that it has been the preserve of the privileged and, as such, subject to much unnecessary pomp and stuffed-shirtedness. As golf has become more popular and, to a degree, less exclusive, some golfers have taken a more fun approach to the game. Take, for instance, golfing idioms, which are often shared among players at a local course and are as colourful and inventive as any pair of Argyle socks.

Author Jack Palmer collects some of the more risqué examples in his book *Politically Incorrect Golf Shots* which, while provocative, follows another great British tradition: that of poking fun at celebrities. So next time you end up with a 'nasty lie', why not call it 'the Tony Blair', or, if you find your ball 'buried in the sand', the King Tut – the possibilities are almost endless and always amusing! Here are some more examples, with their short descriptions:

The Blondie aka the Marilyn Monroe – 'A fair crack up the middle.'
Everyone likes one of these. Keep them coming.

The O. J. Simpson – 'Got away with it.'
Bank it and move on, just don't push your luck – or next time you could wind up in serious trouble.

The Rubber Johnny aka the Condom – 'It was safe, but it didn't feel great.'
Sometimes you have to put safety first to ensure you stay alive.

The Abu Hamza – 'A nasty hook.'
This is often the result of having an iron grip, so check your fundamentals and swing with a smooth tempo.

The General Belgrano – 'It's good to sink a big one.'
Few things boost your confidence as much as sinking a big one in the clutch.

SAY WHAT?

Some interesting turns of phrase associated
with the game:

BAG RAT: derogatory term for a caddy.
FLUB: a bad shot of any sort.
HACKER: someone who ungracefully 'hacks' their
way around the course.
WHIFF: a missed shot.

A married couple are enjoying a round of golf when at the fifth green the husband collapses and starts screaming, 'Help me, Judith, I think I'm having a heart attack!'

His wife reassures him that she'll do everything she can, checks he is comfortable and dashes off to try and find help.

A few minutes later she reappears, picks up her putter and begins sizing up her putt. 'What on earth are you doing?!' cried the man. 'I'm lying here in danger of death and you're carrying on with your game?! I thought you were going to find help?'

'Oh I did, dear. I found a doctor at the second hole – he shouldn't be too long. Everyone agreed to let him play through.'

FORE ELSE!

Golfers love etiquette. There isn't a situation in the world that they couldn't come up with a complex and largely unwritten set of rules for. Sometimes they like to enforce these rules with club legislation and polite but cutting discussions. Sometimes they like to enforce these rules with the nearest blunt object to hand. That was certainly the case with two groups of Washington golfers in 1975, who came to blows over whether the second group had shouted 'fore' or just rudely hit their balls at the first group. What started off as a heated discussion over etiquette evolved into one man hospitalised with a fractured skull, a father and son needing seven stitches apiece, another man being gouged with a shattered golf club and a total of four broken golf clubs. Remember, golfers, shout 'fore' and shout it loudly.

STAR SWINGERS

Tomorrow I hope to golf. Ah me!
Those who have not seen me golf
have indeed missed the Delight
of the Age!

Rudyard Kipling in a letter to his children

A TRIO OF WEDGE-WIELDING WORDSMITHS...

ARTHUR CONAN DOYLE – one of his most memorable tales – *The Hound of the Baskervilles* – was supposedly conceived while the author was away at a golfing weekend at Royal Cromer in 1901. Also, drawing on his spiritualist beliefs, Arthur requested that his son Kingsley, who was due to join the fighting in World War One, meet him on the fourth green at Crowborough Beacon, should he not be able to return in body. Kingsley didn't survive the war, and Arthur could often be seen at Crowborough, lingering at the fourth.

P. G. WODEHOUSE – *Golf Digest* once called him 'the funniest golf writer who ever lived' and he could often be seen at the Sound View Golf Club in Great Neck, New York. During his years of play the eminent author got down to a 16 handicap – which, by anyone's standards, is no joke.

RUDYARD KIPLING – a close friend of Conan Doyle, Kipling was also a golfer – though not as accomplished as Conan Doyle, who once gave him a lesson at Brattleboro, Vermont. Kipling does, however, have a golfing claim to fame: he supposedly invented 'snow golf' while playing in winter in Vermont, trying to sink a red-painted ball into a tin can nestled in the snow.

AUGUSTA LIKES IKE

Augusta has seen some illustrious members in its time, but one who left more than a passing impression is former President Eisenhower. As an Augusta National member Ike spent enough time at the course to have three permanent features named after him. The Eisenhower Tree is a loblolly pine at the seventeenth, which Ike always seemed to hit during play. As such, he suggested in a club meeting that it be removed – however, the tree remains and has grown prouder and taller as the years have gone by. An instance in which the president's suggestion was put into effect was in the creation of what came to be known as Ike's Pond. Eisenhower mentioned to the club's chairman Clifford Roberts that he'd found a good place to build a dam, should the idea of a fishing pond ever be considered. Sure enough, the dam was built and the pond given the president's name. And the Eisenhower Cabin is one of a number at Augusta, built after his inauguration, to Secret Service security standards, at a cost of $75,000 (1950s' money).

For a competitive junky like me, golf is a great solution. Because it smacks you in the face every time you think you have accomplished something.

Michael Jordan

I'm the kind of guy who has to tell his wife he's going to Hooters so he can go play golf.

Ray Romano

LIFE IMITATING ART

One of *Caddyshack*'s biggest stars – Bill Murray – is a keen golfer in real life. Murray, who played the hilariously unhinged greenskeeper Carl Spackler, joins his six brothers, along with other friends of the cause, each year to take part in the annual Murray Bros. Caddyshack Charity Golf Tournament at World Golf Village in Florida. Bill even has a book about golf – *Cinderella Story: My Life in Golf* (1999) – the title of which alludes to the well-known scene in *Caddyshack* in which his character is playing out the fantasy of being a 'young Cinderella', having 'come outta nowhere' to win the Masters – commenting on the series of swings he takes at the flowers in front of him as he goes.

MAMA ZETA

The only female Brit in *Golf Digest*'s 'Hollywood's Top 100 Golfers' list in 2007, Welsh wonder Catherine Zeta-Jones, played in the Mission Hills Star Trophy competition in Hainan, China in 2010.

THE CELEBRITY GOLF TOUR

Forget your Jack Nicholsons and your Alice Coopers – Britain has a celebrity golfing event that boasts more famous faces than you can shake a 5 iron at. The Celebrity Golf Tour brings together British celebs from across the years, from sportsmen to TV personalities, with the proceeds from their tour going to a host of good causes. Registered players are teamed up with a celeb for a day's hard golfing, which is followed by a gala dinner and cabaret performance by some of the famous faces in attendance. If you've ever wondered what Jasper Carrott's short game is like, or if Bruce Forsyth can shake and move on the fairway as well as he can on the ballroom dance floor, you may well get the chance to find out with the Celebrity Golf Tour!

FAMOUS GOLFER: TIGER WOODS (1975–)

He will win more majors than Arnold Palmer and me combined.
Jack Nicklaus on Tiger Woods

The highest earning sportsperson of all time, Eldrick Tont Woods, was born in California; his father Earl was a retired Lieutenant Colonel and Vietnam War veteran, of mixed African-American, Chinese and Native American ancestry. His mother was from Thailand, of Thai, Chinese and Dutch ancestry, and he was brought up as a Buddhist. He began to play golf before the age of two, encouraged by his father who was a keen golfer himself, and the early promise eventually led to junior championships. His nickname came from a Vietnamese soldier friend of his father and by the time he began his achievements in junior and amateur golf, he was already known as 'Tiger' Woods.

In 1996 he turned professional and so began the 'Age of the Tiger'. He signed endorsement deals worth $40 million with Nike, Inc. and $20 million with Titleist, the highest paid contracts in golf history to that stage. He was named *Sports Illustrated*'s 1996 Sportsman of the Year, and began his tradition of wearing a red shirt during the final round of tournaments, a colour he believes symbolises aggression and assertiveness.

His first major championship was clinched at the Masters less than a year later and at the time of writing he has won a total of fourteen major championships, second only to Jack Nicklaus, who won eighteen. Other achievements include holding the world number one spot for the greatest number of weeks both consecutively and in total, being awarded the PGA Player of the Year award a record ten times, and being only the second player along with Nicklaus to win the Grand Slam three times. His fearsome drive has led many golf courses to add yardage to their tees– a practice that became known as 'Tiger-Proofing'.

In 2009 Woods decided to take a break from golf following an international media storm that had sprung up regarding claims of marital infidelity, only returning in time for the 2010 Masters Tournament. However, on the course Tiger Woods continues to do as much as anyone to raise the profile and popularity of golf and if he is playing a tournament, you can be sure the crowds will gather.

Dennis Hopper playing golf is a sure sign of the impending apocalypse.

Kris Kristofferson

SOCIAL HISTORY OF GOLF

Although golf was originally
restricted to wealthy, overweight
Protestants, today it's open to
anybody who owns hideous clothing.

Dave Barry

Golf, although enduringly popular, can never be accused of being a progressive sport. Even as the number of golfers in England and Wales in the 1890s steadily increased, the percentage of those that were *not* male and comfortably middle class remained the same: practically none. At that time a yearly subscription cost £2, more than a week's wages for working-class men and labourers. Compounding the monetary barrier was the trickier issue of class mobility. Any application for membership had to be proposed and seconded, and then voted for by the existing club members. Unsurprisingly, there weren't many middle- and upper-class members eager to let the proletariat into their ranks.

Meanwhile, in Scotland...

Golf was free! Lairds and labourers could play together on the same course. Or at least they could until 1913, when St Andrews started to levy charges for the use of the Old Course.

BITS AND PIECES

- The Cantelupe at Forest Row, Sussex, lays claim to being the first artisan golf club, established in 1892

- It was only in 1962 that the American PGA's controversial by-law stipulating 'Caucasians only' was removed.

- In 1861 the Perth Town Council in Scotland made the mistake of planting more trees on the North Inch golf course. Protesting about the fact that the extra trees would impact their play, the North Inch club members staged a mass riot and tore up the trees. The Town Council decided not to replant.

UNDER FIRE

What do golf fanatics do when there is a war on? Simply use it as excuse to make more rules. In 1941 the Richmond Golf Club realised that World War Two was making it jolly hard to complete a round, and came up with a few extra guidelines:

1. Players are asked to collect bomb and shrapnel splinters to save these causing damage to the mowing machines.
2. In competitions, during gunfire or while bombs are falling, players may take shelter without penalty for ceasing play.
3. The position of known delayed-action bombs are marked by red flags at a reasonable, but not guaranteed, safe distance therefrom.
4. Shrapnel and/or bomb splinters on the fairways or in bunkers, within a club's length of a ball, may be moved without penalty, and no penalty shall be incurred if a ball is thereby caused to move accidentally.
5. A ball moved by enemy action may be replaced or, if lost or destroyed, a ball may be dropped not nearer the hole without penalty.
6. A ball lying in a crater may be lifted and dropped not nearer the hole, preserving the line to the hole, without penalty.
7. A player whose stroke is affected by the simultaneous explosion of a bomb may play another ball. Penalty one stroke.

ILLICIT GOLF

1457 – The Scottish parliament of King James II bans golf, in fear that its subjects were spending too much time on the green and not enough time practising archery.

1470 – Wanting to make sure the Scots knew this was serious, James III banned golf again.

1491 – Clearly at this point James IV had some doubts that the message was getting through. His parliament announced that golf was really, really, no-joking, banned.

1502 – The ban on golf is lifted.

1513 – The Scots are defeated heavily at Flodden Field, dominated by English archers in the first assault.

BUSINESS ETIQUETTE

It's easy enough to blot your card when it comes to course etiquette, but factor in business etiquette and you could be hitting double bogeys all over the place. Doing business on the course is a lucrative game, as long as it's played right.

1. Business should be discussed casually on the course, and closed at the 19th hole.
2. It's not the done thing to talk business before the 5th hole or after the 15th hole.
3. If you have been invited to play, always offer to cover the costs of green fees and any extras that crop up.
4. If you are the one who issued the invitation, be prepared to cover the costs of playing.
5. As the host you should invite your guest to play first at the first hole. Normal golf etiquette of lowest score from the previous hole resumes in the holes following.
6. Only drink alcohol if the host offers it to you, and then stick to only two drinks.
7. No one likes a cheater. If you cheat at golf there is nothing stopping you cheating at business.
8. If you're a bad loser, keep business to the boardroom!
9. If you have a mobile phone or pager switched on, you're not a good golfer. If you use them to conduct other business while your client is with you, you're not a good businessman!
10. Tipping is the charge of the host; however, personal caddies may be tipped by guests.

Show me a good loser and I'll
show you a man who is playing
golf with his boss.

Anonymous

Golf appeals to the idiot and the
child in us. Just how childlike golf
players become is proven by their
frequent inability to count past five.

John Updike

GAME OF A LIFETIME

The youngest ever person to hit a hole-in-one was just three years old. Jake Paine flexed his little muscles and got the shot over a 65-yard hole. How about that, Tiger? The oldest person to hit a hole-in-one was Harold Stilson, a spring chicken at 101. He sank the ball over a 108-yard hole using a 4 iron.

DIEHARD GOLF FANATICS

According to a Swedish scientific study, golfers live five years longer than their peers. The clever Swedes compared data from 30,000 golfers to that of non-golfers of the same sex, age and socio-economic status and found the death rate among the golfers to be 40 per cent lower than it was among the non-golfers over the same period. They also found that practice makes perfect, as those with the lowest handicaps could expect to live the longest.

A PERFECT MATCH

They say that men only have one thing on their minds, one crude obsession that fills their brain from the moment they wake up to the moment they fall asleep. That's right: golf. And with the explosion of the Internet, golfers are able to find like-minded people from all over the world to sate their desires with. Gone are the days of 'golfing guy seeks golfing girl' being tucked away in the 'specialist interests' section of the classified ads. Now there are entire websites, like 'TEE*fore*TWO' and 'DateAGolfer', devoted to lonely golfers seeking someone to tee off with, and maybe more. Who said golf didn't move with the times?

THE GOFF

The first book dedicated entirely to golf was written by Thomas Mathison in 1743 and was titled *The Goff*. It was the fashion of the time to write long mock-heroic poems about not very heroic subjects. Mathison tapped into this craze and combined it with another rising obsession: Goff. He describes the struggle of two young golfers on the Leith links, dreaming of trophies. They are watched over by the dubiously named Goddess Golfinia.

> Goff, and the Man, I sing, who, em'lous, plies,
> The jointed club; whose balls invade the skies;
> Who from Edina's [Edinburgh's] tow'rs, his peaceful home,
> In quest of fame o'er Letha's [Leith's] plains did roam.
> Long toil'd the hero, on the verdant field,
> Strain'd his stout arm the weighty club to wield;
> Such toils it cost, such labours to obtain
> The bays of conquest, and the bowl to gain.

> Thomas Mathison,
> from *The Goff*

PLUS FOURS
AT THE READY

They didn't wear Plus Fours
because they were crack players.
They were crack players because
they wore Plus Fours.

P. G. Wodehouse

NO SKIRTS ON THE COURSE PLEASE

Perhaps you know a golfer who is an absolute stickler for tradition, who sniffs at the player who wanders onto the course in anything but the time-honoured long tailored trouser and shirt with a collar. If so, you might like to see their face when you turn up at the tee in the 'traditional' garb of the original golfer; kilts and animal skins. The Scottish shepherds who supposedly invented golf didn't think to invent a new outfit to play it in and instead played in their normal clothes. Their kilt, or more accurately their 'plaid', was a stretch of material several yards long that they would drape about their torso to protect them from the bitter elements. As your wealth increased, the colours of your plaid grew more bright and jaunty, but it is more likely the earliest golfers were not rich and sported muted hues of brown and cream. Far from the below-the-knee rule of many clubs today, the belted plaid was correctly worn above the knee, so it would just brush the back of the calves when kneeling. If that makes you think of a whole new meaning for wind factor in ball play, don't worry, they wore trews underneath them.

GENTRY DOES IT

By the 1900s the English gentry had a firm grip on the game of golf and dress codes became subject to the fashion of the day. For a while a golfer's swing had to battle with heavy tweed jackets and ruffled cravats. The 1920s saw a burst of popularity for the plus fours, named for the extra four inches added to the normal breeches and heavily influenced by the uniform of the well-to-do British officers of World War One. The additional material of the plus four allowed for a freer range of movement and, we assume, a rapid improvement in the swing. Alas, all good things have to come to an end and, as the 1930s dawned, so did the era of the long trouser. Men of decency played golf and men of decency wore full morning suits. Thus, it became a common sight to see a group of men slogging around the course in suit jacket, shirt and tie, with their heavy trousers tucked into their socks.

BAGGIES OR BREECHES?

In this age of information there is no excuse for getting the dress code on a course wrong. Most clubs have their particular dress code published on their website, helpfully distinguishing between club code and course code. If you are still unsure, or are not an Internet user, you can always phone the club and ask them to clarify the dress code for you.

Here are some general handy hints for what to wear:

1. Classic edition: collared shirt – tucked in – with a pair of long, tailored trousers and golf shoes. Socks must be worn at all times. If you are wearing this outfit it's unlikely there is a course in all the world that will turn you away.
2. Summer edition: collared shirt – tucked in – with a pair of knee-length tailored shorts and golf shoes. Short plain sports socks, or long plain sports socks, worn up, must be worn at all times.
3. Don't edition: Unless you are absolutely sure, do not wear denim on the course or in the clubhouse. Football shirts, or round neck T-shirts are generally a no-no, and hot pants should not be worn by either sex.

The golfing girl of today should indeed be grateful that she need not play in a sailor hat, a high stiff collar, a voluminous skirt and petticoats, a motor veil or a wide skirt with leather binding.

Mabel Stringer

HATS OFF TO SAMMY

Sam Snead is a golfing legend, not only for his so-called 'perfect swing', but also for his image on the course – most notably he regularly wore a straw hat while playing, which gave him a then uncommonly laid-back 'folksy' aspect. To top this off, he was also known to occasionally play his games barefoot.

FANCY PANTS

Gloria Minoprio, in addition to being a keen golfer, was an amateur magician, an unusual combination though perhaps a useful one. She attracted attention during the 1933 English Ladies' Championship by playing with only one club, a trend which has not widely caught on in the succeeding years. More scandalously, during the same championship, she shocked decent society by wearing trousers on the course – tight-fitting navy blue trousers, which she claimed had the advantage over skirts for comfort and practicality. Although The Ladies' Golf Union issued an official statement carefully distancing themselves, we like to think they secretly breathed a sigh of relief that the long, heavy skirts of yesteryear were no more.

SOCKING IT TO 'EM

Often given as stocking fillers at Christmas to
unsuspecting fathers across the land, Argyle socks are
also firm favourites on the golf course. The pattern
itself was derived from the tartan of Clan Campbell,
of course based in Argyll. Pringle of Scotland
popularised the design with its socks and sweaters,
as worn by the Duke of Windsor while playing golf
– hence nowadays Pringle, Argyle socks and golf go
hand in hand.

I hope you're wearing that for a bet.

Colin Montgomerie to Payne Stewart

Golf is a game where white men can dress up as black pimps and get away with it.

Robin Williams

CRAZY GOLF

Do golfers' drives put them crazy
or their putts drive them crazy?

Valerie Ferguson

Regular players of the game will no doubt agree that a seemingly ordinary game of golf can, at any point on any given day, quite easily turn into something infuriating, perhaps as your ball veers wildly off in the wrong direction on a green you were sure was level, or is blown into the broccoli by some freak gust – leaving you wondering whether or not someone has booby-trapped the course as some perverse idea of a joke at your expense. This sort of funny business isn't welcomed by golfers who are out for a serious round, but when the game is minigolf and the zany and extravagant obstacles have been placed in your way on purpose, the more devious the design, the better. Like regular golf, 'crazy golf' requires skilled judgement, precise club control and an ability to keep cool in the face of unexpected challenges – all considerable achievements when, for instance, your ball is taken on a roller coaster ride up conveyor belts, around loops, down spirals, up a clown's nose and out the back end of a fire-breathing dragon before dribbling towards the hole on whichever line it has randomly ended up taking!

NOT-SO-CRAZY BEGINNINGS

Today there are many forms of minigolf, some more ridiculous than others, but the original miniature golf course can still be found at none other than the home of the game itself, St Andrews. The 18-hole course of putting greens, known as the 'Himalayas', was created in 1867 for the benefit of those women who wanted to try their hand at golf but who, in keeping with the social conventions of the time, were not permitted to swing higher than shoulder level.

Once the idea of a miniature course caught on, various establishments started to offer ways for paying customers to enjoy this downsized and simplified version of the real thing. The Americans were the first to take it into mass production with the 1916 'Thistle Dhu' course design at Pinehurst, North Carolina. With minigolf on the rise, enthusiast Thomas McCulloch Fairbairn decided to create a more suitable artificial 'green', which consisted of cottonseed hulls, sand, oil and dye, and with this development the game became even more widespread. Although the Americans were leaders in developing the sport, statistics show that they haven't been so exemplary when it comes to succeeding in competitions – the world ranking list, compiled by the sport's international governing body, the World Minigolf Sport Federation (WMF), is dominated by European players in both female and male categories.

WMF STANDARD COURSES

The WMF has strict guidelines as to what consists of a standard approved minigolf course. These fall into four categories:

MINIATURE GOLF – short holes mostly built using pale-looking Fibre Cement, which gives them the look of obstacles rather than golf holes. Players can't stand on any part of the hole while playing.

FELTGOLF – consists of holes with a felt playing surface and wooden rails, which players may stand on while taking their shot. Often longer and more various than the standard minigolf courses.

CONCRETE – developed by Swiss architect Paul Bogni, this type of course has steel rails and up to eighteen holes.

MINIGOLF OPEN STANDARD (MOS) – more commonly known as 'Adventure Golf' or 'Crazy Golf', MOS courses usually consist of holes lined with artificial grass and can essentially be as wild and wonderful as the owner wishes them to be.

MINIGOLF ON LEGS

If, by some outside chance, crazy golf isn't quite crazy enough for you, why not try your hand at golf billiards? If you're lucky enough to come across an outdoor golf billiards 'course' (perhaps in some remote seaside resort in the nether regions of Wales), you may enjoy using a cue rather than a club to navigate obstacles, similar to those found on a minigolf course, at waist height. Mostly seen as a bit of fun in Europe, golf billiards in America is a little more serious: it has its own set of elaborate rules and is more likely to be played indoors on snooker tables, with players aiming to pot their ball in numbered pockets in the correct order.

PAR-KING MAD

This awe-inspiring adventure golf course started out life as a driving range in Morton Grove, Illinois, before being developed into the Par-King Skill Golf course in the 1960s. Today it's celebrated as the 'Taj Mahal of miniature golf' and has been named in *Golf Digest* as one of the twenty places every golf fan must visit.

Par-King's Statue of Liberty hole features a golden replica of the famous lady, below which there is a water trap with a bridge crossing to the other side; there's also an inspired replica of the Sears Tower, which takes your ball up in its elevator before dropping it off at the hole. Perhaps the most impressive, though, is the course's Rollercoaster hole, resembling a classic American fairground ride, which takes the player's ball up, down and around on its bright red track. The whole thing is inventive minigolf at its best.

BITS AND PIECES

- The Professional Putters Association (PPA) was established in 1959 by Don Clayton, the founder of Putt-Putt Golf (a golf-based family amusement centre chain across America). The organisation was set up to promote and regulate the sport of putting in its own right.

- A company called UrbanCrazy creates bespoke portable crazy golf courses to be set up indoors or outdoors anywhere in the world. The courses are available to rent or buy and have proved highly popular at business shows, exhibitions, parties and team-building events; they've even featured on TV's *A Question of Sport*. In 2011, the crisp company Walkers launched a new range of crinkle-cut crisps, and commissioned a special crinkly-surfaced crazy golf course to promote it, while a miniature golf course in a back garden in London had to be designed to go in and out of a shed.

- The Harris Cup, a well-known miniature golf tournament in the U.S., offers $10,000 to its winner.

- Crazy Farm Golf in Northern Ireland is an 18-hole course designed in the shape of the entire country itself, with three holes in each county. Situated on a working farm, it takes you through the history and culture of Northern Ireland, with authentic farming machinery integrated into the course. Players learn about milling corn in the eighteenth century, the potato famine of the mid 1800s, cattle farming since Neolithic times, cheesemaking and the waterwheel used to mill barley for Bushmills whiskey.

SOME WMF-APPROVED COURSES IN THE UK

Aberdeen – Pirate Island Adventure Golf
Bristol – Jungle Rumble Adventure Golf
Hastings – Planet Hastings Adventure Golf
Hoveton – Wroxham Barns
Margate – Strokes Adventure Golf
Southend-on-Sea – Adventure Island
Worthing – Splash Point Mini Golf

FAMOUS GOLFER: ANNIKA SÖRENSTAM (1970–)

> I know where I'm at on the money list. I'm here to reach my
> own goals, play my own game.
>
> Annika Sörenstam

The Swedish-American superstar Annika Sörenstam – so much
a part of the modern game of golf she is often simply referred to
as 'Annika' – is not only arguably the best female golfer ever,
but also one of the best golfers the game has ever seen. Her
professional career has seen her win an unbelievable seventy-
two LPGA tournaments and make history by following in the
footsteps of Babe Zaharias and competing in the men's PGA tour
in 2003 at the Bank of America Colonial tournament.

Twin sister to Charlotta (also a successful pro golfer), Annika
was born in Bro, near Stockholm. Like many golfing legends she
was a childhood champion, with a first handicap of 54, though
being a shy girl she often used to deliberately miss putts so she
didn't have to face the limelight. Gaining confidence, Annika

immersed herself in golf, becoming a member of the Swedish national team and winning the title of World Amateur Champion in 1992, at which point she turned pro. At the 1995 U.S. Open Annika won her first LPGA title, going on to win again the following year to become the first non-American golfer to gain two consecutive wins at the Women's Open.

Annika continued to top money lists and dominate her rivals in the early 2000s.

Her appearance on the 2003 men's PGA tour was not without controversy, though crowds cheered her through the tournament until she eventually missed the cut despite some top-notch driving. She continued to add to her scores of accolades and achievements, being ranked the number one female golfer in the first Women's World Golf Rankings. Having just about won everything there is to win in golf several times over, Annika announced her retirement in 2008. Her very own golf school, The ANNIKA Academy, was set up just before she bowed out of the game, with her old coach Henri Reis as head instructor. Like many veterans, her name is now a prestigious commercial brand, continuing to stand for excellence and outstanding, perhaps unmatchable, achievement.

You can take a man's wife. You can even take his wallet. But never on any account take his putter.

Archie Compston

I find it helpful to inform an opponent who's lining up a four-foot putt that under the metric system widely used in other countries, it's actually a putt of just over 1,200 millimetres.

Leslie Nielsen

THE LIGHTER SIDE
OF GOLF

You're supposed to play it for fun,
but the less times you hit the ball,
the more fun you have.

Lou Graham

Perhaps because of the level of skill and concentration it requires, in some circles golf is considered to be a rather serious game – not least because it inspires veterans like Colin Montgomerie to fly off the handle and berate some innocent bystander for coughing, or to curse the wind, his club or anything else within shouting distance. While scenes of intense frustration are never far away on the golf course – especially at the professional level – they are often balanced by equally enthusiastic bouts of laughter and tomfoolery. In fact, more than your average slow-tempo, high-stress sports, golf has resulted in some outstanding humour, be it on the silver screen in movies like *Happy Gilmore* or The Three Stooges' *Three Little Beers*, on the printed page in all-too-true cartoons and comic strips, or simply on the course with friends sharing a laugh with a racy euphemism or two.

WEBSTER'S CLASSIC CARTOONS

Due to its popular appeal, golf has always been a favourite subject for artists and illustrators and, while many stately paintings have been painstakingly produced to show the sport's illustrious history, modern artists have often taken a more light-hearted approach. With a classy caricature-like style, Bilston, West Midlands-born cartoonist Tom Webster, drew sports cartoons – specialising in golf, horseracing and cricket – for the *Daily Mail* and the *Evening Standard* in the 1920s. He had taught himself to draw while working in a railway booking office, and won a newspaper cartoon contest in 1904. His stint at the *Mail* would last twenty years, during which time he made friends with then Arsenal manager Herbert Chapman through a mutual love of golf and, as some accounts suggest, it was Webster's combination of clothing in one of their meetings that inspired Chapman to request white sleeves on his team's red shirts. Many of Webster's cartoons focused on rivalries between certain teams or players, making clever quips in the style of political cartoons – no doubt he would struggle to find a similarly sophisticated caption for some of the scandals that take place on and off the course in today's game!

What a terrible round of golf.
I only hit two good balls today, and
that was when I stood on a rake.

Jimmy Tarbuck

Jim was playing the worst round of his life. Turning to his opponent, Stewart, a much more experienced golfer, he asked how he could turn his game around.

'Well, in your shoes I would shorten your clubs by about six inches,' Stewart volunteered.

'Will that really help?' asked Jim.

'No,' replied Stewart. 'But it will make it easier to fit them in the bin.'

DOTY'S DUFFERS

Award-winning American cartoonist Roy Doty served as an illustrator in World War Two before turning his hand to comic strips. Aside from his 'Wordless Workshop' strip, a light-hearted take on practical DIY tips, he has created a number of cartoons featuring hapless golfers Duffer and Hack, characters Doty has used to explore the more laughable aspects of the game. One cartoon sees them getting 'booked' by a course ranger for taking too long, 'doing five hours in a four-hour zone'.

A duffer sends an errant slice careening through the trees and onto the next fairway, narrowly missing another golfer's head.

The underperforming golfer shyly wanders over to retrieve his ball, at which point the guy who had nearly ended up with a lump on his head starts shouting angrily.

'I'm so sorry,' the duffer says, 'I just didn't have time to shout "FORE".'

'That's funny,' the man replied, 'because you had plenty of time to shout "B*$£!@%S".'

BITS AND PIECES

- *Donald's Golf Game*, a film featuring the well-loved sailor-suit-wearing Disney character, was released in 1938. In it Donald is plagued by his caddies Huey, Dewey and Louie while he contends with his bad luck and a bag of trick clubs.

- *How to Play Golf* was released by Disney in 1944, this time featuring gormless 'dog' Goofy. The hapless hound listens to the narrator's instructions on how to play, but of course gets it all backwards.

- Joe Lee created the beautifully designed Disney Magnolia Golf Course as part of the Disney World Resort in Florida. More than 1,500 magnolia trees line the course.

I don't have an image or a nickname. Maybe I should dye my hair peroxide blonde and call myself The Great White Tadpole.

Ian Woosnam

Sam Snead has a terrific pair of legs. He's double-jointed. He can stand flat-footed in a room and kick an eight-foot ceiling.

Lee Trevino

URBAN GOLFING

I have taught golf at a
driving range for some time and
have seen many people actually
practising mistakes.

Mel Flanagan

In the days when golf first emerged as a serious outdoor sport, no doubt those players at St Andrews relished the bracing winds coming off the sea – what better way to indulge in a bit of friendly competition while getting a healthy dose of the outdoors? And away from the links, golf was somewhat restricted back then to country estates and plus-four-wearing gadabouts. But in the modern age we demand access to everything at all times, regardless of our location or circumstance; hence, we now have golf simulators that can offer a virtual golf experience as accurate as the one you'd get if playing for real, and of course the ubiquitous golf video games for every platform imaginable, from home systems to handheld devices. As green and pleasant areas become either more exclusive or are replaced by ever-expanding cities, it seems logical that golf has been brought out of the woods and into the warm, dry and comfortable indoor environment.

UP ON MANIAC HILL

Aside from miniature golf, one of the first attempts at making the golfing experience less of an all-out, all-day affair was in the introduction of driving ranges. Pinehurst Resort in North Carolina claims to have America's first driving range, set up in the 1930s by Donald Ross. It was called Maniac Hill – perhaps because golfers practising their drives tended to let loose in a manner that might have appeared wild or manic, or perhaps because those who were practising their swing were prone to mutter incomprehensibly after a particularly bad shot. This of course was intended as a way of sharpening up one's drive out of the scenario of a full-length game, though for more and more people – who perhaps don't have the means or the opportunity to play a full round at a pleasant golf club – visiting the driving range is a pursuit in itself, a quick fix or a bit of fun. Just like the pitch and putt, it offers the chance to play golf when space, time and money are constraints.

PENTHOUSE PUTTERS

When you think of New York City, you might conjure images of hot dogs, the Statue of Liberty, yellow-and-black taxis and, of course, high-rise buildings. Golf, surely, does not spring to mind straight away. However, the Big Apple does in fact have a long history of golf – rooftop golf, that is. As the miniature golf craze swept the nation in the 1920s, dozens of rooftop putting courses appeared hundreds of feet above street level. Today, with more high-rises than ever, rooftop putting greens and miniature golf courses are likely to be set up by wealthy residents and building owners who fancy working on their short game on a clear night. In June 2010 Annika Sörenstam joined two PGA pros in New York to take part in the Ultimate Rooftop Golf Challenge: drive a ball from the roof of a forty-storey building on Waterside Plaza into a floating bullseye target on the surface of the East River. The event was organised to raise money for the families of America's Armed Services.

SWINGING SOHO

London is renowned for its classy clubs, and its golf clubs are no exception. However, the Urban Golf club in Soho is not your average 18-hole course – in fact, it's all enclosed in a converted former printworks, with two floors and 6,000 square feet of indoor golfing experience. Combining all the class of a swanky clubhouse – with its vintage leather chairs and chic cocktail bar and lounge – with high-tech simulators and putting 'hallways' that look like art galleries with green carpets, Urban Golf offers its own unique golfing experience for when the jaunt out to the country isn't possible. It has two sister clubs in Kensington and Smithfield, each of which offers a slightly different take on the indoor experience.

VIRTUAL GOLF

Like other professional sports, golf has had many incarnations in the world of video games. Here's a short list of some of the more memorable ones:

Golf, Nintendo (1984) – this 8-bit wonder featured a character that looked distinctly like Super Mario and was one of the first games to feature a power meter to control the strength of a player's shot.

Will Harvey's Zany Golf, Electronic Arts (1988) – took players through a series of crazy golf holes with various novelty obstacles, including a pinball hole which was set up with flippers and bumpers, and a magic-carpet hole in which the player controlled the direction of the ball with the control pad or mouse.

Tiger Woods '99, Electronic Arts (1998) – Tiger's meteoric rise to fame naturally had to be cashed in on by developing a series of video games with his name on them. This particular game featured what were for the time realistic player graphics – it also featured recorded voice comments from Tiger himself and an out-of-place hip hop-style soundtrack.

Outlaw Golf, Simon & Schuster Interactive (2002) – this had a rather novel system of gauging your shot: a composure meter showed how frustrated a player's character was – the more shots you missed, the more you lost composure and the less competent your stroke became. To regain composure, one option was to beat your caddy at the next hole.

Aqua Teen Hunger Force Zombie Ninja Pro-Am, Midway (2007) – a hybrid kart racing, fighting and golfing game featuring characters from the *Aqua Teen Hunger Force* TV show – as ridiculous and redundant as it sounds.

THE PERFECT PUTT

Man has always looked to technology to enhance his abilities, and golf is no exception. Putting machines, which allow golfers to practise their putting stroke in a small space indoors, have been around for a number of years. The most basic of these machines will simply consist of a mechanical unit with a target area and a returning mechanism that shoots your ball back to you. At the other end of the scale there are machines like the Perfect Putting Machine by Z Factor, apparently used by PGA players. This allows you to perfect your putting by guiding your stroke on a rail – which means you get a feel for the proper weighting and length of a good stroke.

GOLFING IN THE ELEMENTS

I played as much golf as I could
in North Dakota, but summer up
there is pretty short. It usually
falls on Tuesday.

Mike Morley

It is not raining rain today –
Those droplets that you see
Are fairly figments of the mind;
It's dry as dry can be.

It is not lightning light today –
That rumbling that you hear
Is just assurance positive
That soon it will be clear.

It is not snowing snow today –
Those softly falling flakes
Will serve to keep us safe and warm
Within our snug windbreaks.

It is not sleeting sleet today –
Those icicles so clear
Are but the promise of the sun
Which shortly will appear.

For when it rains and blows and sleets
All golfers know it's clearing –
We wives who try to spoil their meets
Might just as well stop fearing.

Anna Pettit Broomell, 'Golf Weather'

INTREPID GOLFERS

Golf is one of the few sports which can be played in less than clement weather. Golfers are some of the most intrepid sportsmen, dragging out their clubs and chequered jumpers come torrential rain, gale-force winds or shine. This sort of dogged determination is especially admirable on courses along the Scottish coastline, as sea mists, or 'haars', can blow in at any time, obscuring views and rendering serious play futile for several days at a time. The Ailsa course at the Turnberry Resort in Scotland may be ranked as Britain's number one golf course, but is also prone to some of Scotland's worst weather; the Ailsa rock, a mile out to sea, after which the course is named, is often completely obscured by the dark clouds and heavy rainfall which frequent the area.

RISE TO THE CHALLENGE

Bad weather can make a game of golf exciting, challenging and more fun. Each shot you make will be affected by the conditions, and will cause you to change the way you play, try new things and learn more about your game. Stormy weather is the perfect time to stretch yourself, explore your limits and improve your game. Many professional golfers use 'bad weather days' as an extra opportunity to practise, making sure they will be able to hold their own in competitions should the weather turn sour. Nick Faldo claims that weather shouldn't put off a good player; that you should create your own luck in the wind and rain through good decision-making, determination and bottle.

When the ducks are walking, you know it is too windy to be playing golf.

Dave Stockton

If you are caught on a golf course during a storm and are afraid of lightning, hold up a one iron. Not even God can hit a one iron.

Lee Trevino

Two men are out playing golf. They get to the 17th tee, which overlooks a small lake, and see two guys out on the lake fishing. One says, 'Hey, check out these two idiots fishing in the rain!'

A TURBULENT GAME

One of the worst storms to ever hit a professional golf tournament was at the 1938 Open at Royal St George's. Of the thirty-seven players there, only thirteen broke 80. On the third day, the storm completely destroyed the exhibition tent, causing merchandise and debris to fly across the course, landing up to a mile away. The competition was won by Reg Whitcombe, with a final round score of 78 – the second highest professional final-round score ever.

THE SUN HAS GOT HIS HAT ON...

Playing in the glorious sunshine can be one of life's great pleasures, but it can still pose a threat to the unwary golfer. Research suggests that golf players and fans are more at risk of skin cancer due to lengthy periods of sun exposure. Make sure you apply suncream every couple of hours to any exposed areas of skin, and don't forget to use protective lip balms, and wear sunglasses and, of course, that all-important golfer's hat! Playing golf in extreme heats can also be taxing on the body. Make sure you stay hydrated and dress appropriately to avoid sunstroke.

WHEN THE WIND BLOWS

In strong winds, spin or side on a ball is going to be greatly magnified, and, depending on the direction of the wind, can either greatly reduce or massively increase your ball's speed and trajectory. Try to keep your ball low to avoid crosswinds taking it off course, or, if the wind is in your favour, use less force but aim your ball high so it is carried on the wind. You'll need to keep a wider stance than normal too – there are many embarrassing tales of the unsuspecting golfer blown over mid-swing, and they're sure not to be soon forgotten!

WHEN IT RAINS IT POURS

Wet weather can seriously affect your game, not least because of the difficulty of keeping your eyes open in the pouring rain. Your feet will sink further into the ground, so you'll need to adjust your stance and grip to accommodate this. Wet grass from the rough can get between your club and your ball, affecting the angle and power of your shot. Your shot won't carry as far, and your ball will roll less than normal, if at all, so be prepared to accept that you will make some bad shots and that your game will take longer in the rain. If it's really bucketing down, a fashionable plastic poncho and umbrella-hat ought to do the trick.

EXTREME GOLF

Don't let snow or ice put you off – in Greenland, snow golf is extremely popular, and they even hold an annual World Ice Golf Championship – although the course shape changes every year as the ice reforms!

BE PREPARED

If you do decide to brave the stormy weather, at least go out prepared. You can buy high-tech waterproof and wind-resistant golf suits which, teamed with a couple of under layers, should keep you cosy and dry. Don't forget your golf rain gloves, which will provide extra grip and warmth, and take a couple of towels to make sure your hands, gloves and clubs are as dry as possible before each shot. You can get apps on your phone to tell you the weather conditions for individual courses, such as wind speed and direction. Finally, it is probably worth investing in a home/office golf putting mat – for when the weather really *is* that bad.

WEATHER RULES

- The rules of golf state that bad weather is not a good enough reason to stop play. The only circumstance which constitutes a legitimate reason for play to be discontinued is the risk of lightning.

- In the rain, a player is permitted to use an umbrella while putting, but is not allowed to have someone else hold it.

- Snow and natural ice (but not frost) can be treated as either loose impediments or casual water, at the discretion of the player. This means you have the option of sweeping the snow away or dropping your ball at the outermost limits of the 'casual water' which your ball last crossed and going from there.

GOLF AND
THE MEDIA

I would like to thank the press
from the heart of my bottom.

Nick Faldo after winning The Open in 1992

The game of golf has always created a buzz and excitement. From its early days when it was an emerging sport, right up to the present day where it has become a multi-million pound international industry, it has turned heads. What makes the game continue to be so popular is open to debate, but one thing is for sure – it enjoys plenty of media coverage in a host of live TV broadcasts which have avid fans staying up to all hours to follow the action live, as well as a plethora of magazines and radio broadcasts to keep fans informed.

There is, quite simply, a lot to say about golf – it is, after all, a complicated game that demands that every aspect of play and equipment be developed to a high degree to achieve success. For sports reporters the world over this is very good news; yet the relationship between players and the people commenting on their antics on and off the course has not been without its problems.

TIGER LOSES HIS STRIPES

Tiger Woods – a golfing legend before his mid twenties and one of professional sport's biggest names ever – went from saint to sinner in the space of a week, disappointing millions of fans and undermining years of hard work when in 2010 it was revealed that he had had numerous affairs outside of wedlock. This was not the first, and surely will not be the last, scandal within the game of golf, but what made it so shocking was that in the eyes of the media Tiger was a miracle – endlessly talented, often charismatic and a family man (he honoured his dad and named him as his inspiration for success), not to mention that he was an African-American succeeding in a sport which didn't exactly have a history of black champions. He was a media darling. Then came the revelation of his unfaithfulness, reports of domestic disputes and eventually divorce from his wife Elin Nordegren, all of which sent his fans and the press reeling. The media had built Tiger up as the ideal sportsman, and perhaps because of this his fall from grace was all the more devastating.

THERE'S SOMETHING ABOUT MONTY

Everybody knows Monty – and everybody knows that he's got an explosive temper akin to that of a silverback in mating season. Rather than internalising his anger and frustration on the course, Monty simply lets it out, disregarding the fact that he is being watched by hundreds of spectators and whole teams of TV camera people and other broadcasters. Known for outbursts of verbal abuse and sometimes violence, flying off the handle has become his trademark – in the 1991 Ryder Cup, for instance, he stormed onto the 18th green from the gallery and proceeded to jab Ian Poulter in the chest with his long putter, giving him a bruised rib. Monty's hot-headedness has even been parodied in a television advert for KitKat, which makes fun of being touchy about noises from the crowd while players are putting – something that has caused numerous fits of rage for Colin Montgomerie – and sees him inadvertently distract a fellow golfer during a high-pressure putt by snapping off a finger of the chocolate bar. Chances are that if a collection of Monty's press shots were to be compiled, at least three quarters would show him with the look of blue murder on his contorted face.

BIG HITTER

In America, many things are bigger and, on the odd occasion, this means they are also better – and *Golf Digest* is almost certainly the world's biggest golf magazine. Every golfer knows *Golf Digest*, because it's been built up as the dominant media force in the world of golf journalism – it publishes lists like 'America's 100 Greatest Golf Courses' and also ranks those outside of America, all decided by a panel of several hundred golf experts. In this respect the magazine is almost like a governing body in itself, something that few sports publications anywhere can boast.

GOLF MONTHLY

Although *Golf Digest* is arguably the biggest golf magazine out there, the UK's *Golf Monthly* lays claim to being the oldest golfing monthly in the world. It was started in 1911 by double Open champion Harold Hilton, who hailed from West Kirby, Wirral. He was one of the few amateurs ever to have won an Open – once in 1892 and again in 1897. Being a golf writer himself, Hilton was determined to provide a magazine that was written by golfers, for golfers. *Golf Monthly* was the result, and it is still going strong a hundred years later.

GOLF'S GOLDEN TV MOMENTS

Golf has been covered on TV for decades, and for those who can't make it to the big tournaments it can provide a spectacle that is almost as tense and compelling as being there in person – with enthusiastic outbursts from commentators and an often ecstatic crowd, history is made on the course and recorded through the eye of the TV camera. Here's a list of some memorable golf coverage over the years:

1962 OPEN CHAMPIONSHIP – Arnold Palmer wins at Royal Troon – an impressive win and some memorable footage from the early days of golf coverage on TV.

1986 MASTERS – a 'washed up' Jack Nicklaus, aged forty-five, 160th on the money list, came from six shots behind Seve Ballesteros to win, cheered on by a raucous crowd. An emotional moment for all involved and surely one of the greatest moments in golf. As one commentator put it: 'the bear came out of hibernation.'

1991 RYDER CUP – dubbed 'The War on the Shore' by the press, an explosive showdown took place between American Hale Irwin and German Bernhard Langer. Langer crumbled at the last, pushing his short putt right and allowing Team USA to take the win by one stroke.

1996 MASTERS – Tiger plays his first major as a pro and annihilates his elders by winning by twelve shots, becoming the youngest player to win the tournament. The world of golf was stunned, inspiring comments like Tom Watson's, who described Woods as 'the type of player who comes around once in a millennium'.

2000 U.S. OPEN – Tiger Woods put in one of his best performances to win the Open at Pebble Beach by a record fifteen shots. The Golf Channel's Brandel Chamblee called it 'art personified'.

TEE TALK

Golf tips are like aspirin.
One may do you good, but if you
swallow the whole bottle you'll be
lucky to survive.

Harvey Penick

Sex is like money, golf and beer –
even when it's bad, it's good.

Jimmy Williams

I always ask my caddy to tell me
two things: the yardage, and that
I'm the best in the world.

Jack Nicklaus

Men chase golf balls when they're too old to chase anything else.

Groucho Marx

Golf is not a sport. Golf is men in ugly pants, walking.

Rosie O'Donnell

Golf and cricket are the only two games where you can actually put on weight while playing them.

Tommy Docherty

RESOURCES

PUBLICATIONS AND ONLINE RESOURCES

Golf World Magazine

Golf Digest

Golf Monthly

Today's Golfer

www.golftoday.co.uk
www.onlinegolf.co.uk
www.golfblogger.co.uk
www.nationalclubgolfer.com

BOOKS

Chumley, Jim *Golf's Funniest Jokes* (2009, Summersdale Publishers)

Griffin, Fred and Mann, Ralph *Swing Like a Pro: The Breakthrough Scientific Method of Perfecting your Golf Swing* (1999, Broadway Books)

Jacklin, Tony and Sieger, Robin *Silent Mind Golf: How to Get Out of Your Own Way and Play Golf Intuitively and Instinctively* (2010, Aurum Press)

Malone, Aubrey *Golfing Wit* (2007, Summersdale Publishers)

Murray, Bill and Peper, George *Cinderella Story: My Life in Golf* (2005, Sanctuary Publishing)

Newell, Steve *The Golf Instruction Manual* (2001, Dorling Kindersley Publishers Ltd)

Palmer, Jack *Politically Incorrect Golf Shots* (2011, Summersdale Publishers)

Ward, Andrew *Golf's Strangest Rounds: Extraordinary But True Golf Stories from Over a Century of Golfing History* (1999, Robson Books)

Woods, Tiger *Tiger Woods: How I Play Golf* (2004, Little, Brown Book Group)

ORGANISATIONS

www.usga.org – The USGA's official website

www.randa.org – The online home of the R&A

www.pga.info – Professional Golfers' Association website

www.englishwomensgolf.org – English Women's Golf Association website